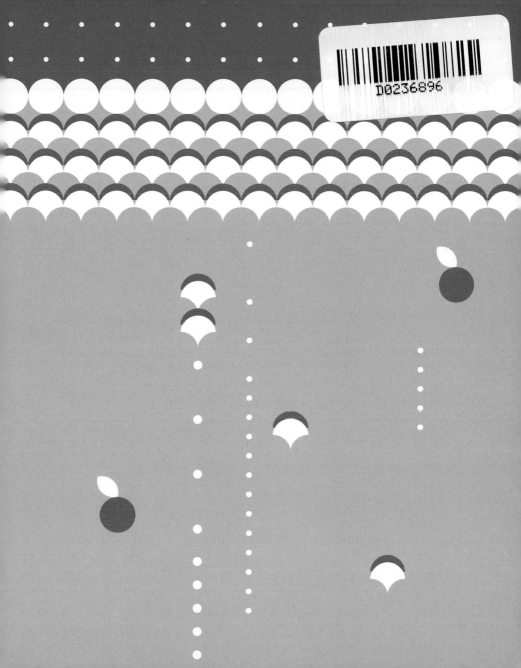

THE COCKTAIL

the cocktail

200 FABULOUS DRINKS

JANE ROCCA

Drawings by Kat Macleod

APPLE

This book is dedicated to Matthew Jacques Rocca

First published in the UK in 2008 by
Apple Press
7 Greenland Street
London NW1 0ND
www.apple-press.com

Reprinted in 2009

Published in Australia in 2005 by
Hardie Grant Books
85 High Street
Prahran, Victoria
3181, Australia
www.hardiegrant.com.au

Text © Jane Rocca 2005
Illustrations © Kat Macleod 2005

ISBN 978-1-84543-257-7

Design by Simone Elder
Index by Fay Donlevy

Printed and bound in China by C&C Offset Printing

3 5 7 9 10 8 6 4 2

CONTENTS

GLASS TYPES

Martini glass

This glass has a triangle-bowl design with a long stem, and is used for a wide range of straight-up (without ice) cocktails, including martinis, manhattans, metropolitans and gimlets. It's perfect for strong drinks and strong personalities.

Highball glass

A tall, straight-sided glass used for long drinks. Highball glasses are generally used to serve light spirits.

Collins glass

Shaped like a highball glass but taller, the Collins glass was originally used for the line of Collins gin drinks. It's now used for tropical and exotic cocktails.

Tumbler

A glass that traditionally has a rounded bottom and is used to serve dark spirits.

Champagne flute

This is ideal for cocktail drinks whose key ingredients include champagne or wine.

Pilsner glass

A tall, footed glass generally used to serve beer.

Coupette glass

This slightly larger, rounded approach to a martini glass has a broad rim for holding salt — ideal for margaritas. It's also used for daiquiris.

Shot glass

Usually used for straight booze. It's a small glass, holding about 30 ml.

Old-fashioned glass

Also known as the rocks glass, this is a short, round glass suitable for drinks served on the rocks. It's for the serious drinker within.

Whisky sour glass

This glass is stemmed, with a wide opening. It's a small version of a Champagne flute.

Liqueur glass

A small, stemmed glass for serving rich liqueurs.

Hurricane glass

A tall and elegant glass named for its resemblance to a hurricane lamp. It's mostly used for exotic cocktails.

Goblet

A drinking glass that has a base and stem.

Absinth glass

A traditional glass used to serve absinth, often a port or small wine glass, usually with engraving around the glass.

Bamboo glass

A glass designed by May Wong that represents the curvature of a natural bamboo structure.

The Cocktail

NOTES

MUDDLING

In a nutshell, when a recipe requires you to muddle an ingredient, you need a wooden pestle to crush them or break them down. Fruit, herbs and sugar are often muddled to unleash flavour or create a paste.

INFUSING SPIRITS

Many spirits now come in different flavours, but some recipes will require some homemade infusions.

You can flavour the alcohol in two ways:

Infusion/maceration:

Place the ingredients with the alcohol in an air-tight container until the flavour is absorbed to your liking (a few days). Store the container at room temperature, out of direct sunlight. You will need to check the infusion every day as after a week the alcohol can take on a stale or bitter flavour, depending on the ingredient.

Pan infusion:

Heat the alcohol in a saucepan with the ingredients until it simmers. Let it sit for up to three hours, then strain alcohol into its original bottle. This method is only suitable for fruit- and sugar-based infusions – not flowers.

champagne chic

There's nothing quite like a glass of bubbly; it's the perfect social lubricant, helping you on your tipsy way as you mingle with friends (and dark strangers). But Champagne conjures romanticism of an old-world kind as well: gorgeous evening gowns and Champagne flutes sparkling at the surface, held aloft by delicate, feminine wrists.

Champagne is dreamlike, forthrightly sophisticated and ever so womanly. It's the ultimate accessory for when you're looking your glammed-up best.

It might be considered the flirty, giddy staple, tottering around on heels, but Champagne also has substance and body. It's the leggy blonde who also boasts a degree in Neuroscience. Champagne can be tingly and sweet, fruity or simply brut dry — the flavours taking you on all sorts of journeys — as versatile and varied as those who drink it.

The Bellini is a peachy classic one mustn't pass up, but those hell-bent on the weightiness of beer should opt for the Black Velvet, steeped in creamy, frothy Guinness. However indulged, Champagne is for girls who just want to have fun, for those nights tinged with debauchery and that certain sparkle of life.

CLASSIC CHAMPAGNE COCKTAIL
Champagne flute

INGREDIENTS
sugar cube
2 dashes of Angostura bitters
90 ml Champagne
20 ml cognac
twist of lemon
slice of orange to garnish

METHOD
Soak sugar cube with Angostura
bitters in a Champagne flute.
Add Champagne and cognac,
squeeze in a twist of lemon and
garnish with half a slice of orange.

BLACK VELVET

Champagne flute

INGREDIENTS

90 ml Guinness Stout
90 ml Champagne

METHOD

Fill half a flute with Guinness. Float an equal part of Champagne on top.

MORNING GLORY

Champagne flute

INGREDIENTS

75 ml chilled Champagne
75 ml orange juice
15 ml triple sec
orange wheel to garnish

METHOD

Fill three-quarters of a flute with Champagne, add orange juice and triple sec, and then garnish with an orange wheel.

CAROLINA
Wine glass

INGREDIENTS
60 ml Strega
60 ml Champagne

METHOD
Pour Strega into a chilled wine glass, add Champagne and stir slightly.

FLIRTINI
Martini glass

INGREDIENTS
2 pieces of fresh pineapple
15 ml Cointreau
15 ml vodka
30 ml pineapple juice
90 ml Champagne
cherry to garnish

METHOD
Muddle the pineapple pieces and Cointreau. Add vodka and pineapple juice, then stir. Strain into a chilled martini glass and top with Champagne. Garnish with a cherry and serve.

CHERRY CHAMPAGNE
Champagne flute

INGREDIENTS
120 ml Champagne
45 ml cherry brandy

METHOD
Combine ingredients in a
Champagne flute and serve.

FRENCH 75
Collins glass

INGREDIENTS

60 ml sour mix
45 ml cognac
150 ml Champagne

METHOD

Combine sour mix and cognac in a
Collins glass with a little ice, and stir.
Fill with Champagne, then garnish
with a French flag!

BELLINI
Champagne flute

INGREDIENTS

30 ml fresh peach puree or nectar
90 ml Champagne
peach slices to garnish

METHOD

Pour peach puree into a Champagne
flute. Gently top with Champagne and
garnish with a fresh peach slice.

KIR ROYALE

Champagne flute

INGREDIENTS

30 ml crème de cassis
150 ml Champagne

METHOD
Pour crème de cassis into a flute and
gently pour Champagne on top.

CHAMPAGNE ROYALE

Champagne flute

INGREDIENTS

splash of black raspberry liqueur
180 ml Champagne
fresh raspberries to garnish

METHOD

Pour liqueur into a flute, then slowly
fill with Champagne. Garnish with
raspberries.

MARTINI ROYALE

Martini glass

INGREDIENTS

90 ml chilled vodka or gin
90 ml Champagne

METHOD

Pour vodka or gin into a chilled martini
glass and top with Champagne.

FRAISE DE CHAMPAGNE
Champagne flute

INGREDIENTS
100 ml Champagne
30 ml crème de fraise des bois
15 ml cognac

METHOD
Combine alcohol in a Champagne
flute and serve.

LEMON CELEBRATION
Champagne flute

INGREDIENTS
30 ml black raspberry liqueur
30 ml Bacardi Limon
90 ml Champagne

METHOD
Shake ingredients gently with ice
(the Champagne will fizz).
Strain into a Champagne flute.

AMERICAN ROSE
Wine glass

INGREDIENTS
45 ml brandy
½ tsp Pernod
1 tsp grenadine
90 ml Champagne
peach slice to garnish

METHOD
Shake brandy, Pernod and grenadine,
and strain into a chilled wine glass.
Fill with Champagne and garnish with
a peach slice.

CAMPARI CHAMPAGNE

Champagne flute

INGREDIENTS

30 ml Campari
120 ml Champagne
twist of lemon peel to garnish

METHOD

Pour Campari into a flute and fill
with Champagne. Twist the lemon
peel over the drink and serve.

A GOODNIGHT KISS

Champagne flute

INGREDIENTS

drop of Angostura bitters
sugar cube
120 ml Champagne
splash of Campari

METHOD

Place a drop of Angostura bitters on
a sugar cube and set in a Champagne
flute. Add Champagne and Campari.

sipping at the sin palace

Gin sounds so old-fashioned, doesn't it? It's so proper and prim-school like. If it had a wardrobe it would be full of pleated skirts and ruffled shirts, lots of tweed and brooches. If gin were a girl she'd come across a little bashful and not quite willing to explore her princess qualities – but if she only knew what was hiding under her petticoat … She's a little prudish, but there's a diva dying for exposure underneath that veil of reservation.

If gin were a literary club, it would be packed with Emily Brontë and Jane Austen bookworms. Gin is for hopeless romantics, clinging to the ideal of Heathcliff waiting out yonder to take them away.

The gin and tonic is a classic drink - so ladylike, so petal-sweet and mildly snobbish. After a starring appearance in the mid-century as an oh-so-stylish martini, gin disappeared for a while. But now this spirit has been ripped away from its mothballs to seduce a whole new generation.

EMMA PEEL MARTINI
Martini glass

INGREDIENTS
30 ml gin
15 ml apple schnapps
15 ml watermelon liqueur
15 ml apple juice
15 ml watermelon juice
apple peel to garnish

METHOD
Shake and strain all ingredients into
a chilled martini glass. Garnish with
green apple spiral (left floating).

CIN GIN
Martini glass

INGREDIENTS
½ fresh cinnamon stick
splash of pineapple juice
60 ml gin
5 ml lemongrass and ginger tea
cinnamon stick to garnish

METHOD
Muddle cinnamon with pineapple juice,
then add gin and ice. Shake and stir.
Serve in a martini glass laced with
lemongrass and ginger tea. Garnish
with cinnamon stick.

BOMBAY SCHMINT
Martini glass

INGREDIENTS
6 mint leaves
60 ml gin
15 ml crème de peche
dash of orange juice
sprig of mint to garnish

METHOD
Muddle mint leaves. Combine with
other ingredients, shake and strain
into a martini glass. Garnish with a
mint sprig.

GIN GARDEN
Martini glass

INGREDIENTS
2-3 chunks cucumber
15 ml elderflower cordial
45 ml gin
45 ml apple juice
cucumber slice to garnish

METHOD
Muddle cucumber with elderflower
cordial. Shake with remaining
ingredients and serve straight up in
a chilled martini glass. Garnish with
a cucumber slice.

ALOE VERA MARTINI
Martini glass

INGREDIENTS
50 ml gin
15 ml aloe vera water
10 ml crème de peche
twist of orange to garnish

METHOD
Shake and strain all ingredients
into a martini glass. Garnish with
a twist of orange.

CAMPANA
Martini glass

INGREDIENTS
30 ml gin
15 ml Campari
15 ml sweet vermouth
10 ml lime juice
15 ml sugar syrup
slice of lime to garnish

METHOD
Shake and strain all ingredients into
a chilled martini glass then garnish
with a slice of lime.

CLASSIC MARTINI

Martini glass

INGREDIENTS

50 ml gin
5 ml dry vermouth
cocktail olive to garnish

METHOD

Stir gin and vermouth with ice cubes
in a mixing glass until chilled. Then
strain into a chilled martini glass.
Garnish with a cocktail olive.

POMEGRANATE MARTINI

Martini glass

INGREDIENTS

4 tsp pomegranate seeds
mint leaf
10 ml passionfruit puree
60 ml gin
5 ml grenadine

METHOD

Muddle pomegranate, mint and puree,
add gin and grenadine, shake and
double-strain into a martini glass.

THE MARTINI THAT WON THE 1951 MARTINI COMPETITION IN CHICAGO

Martini glass

INGREDIENTS
15 ml dry vermouth
90 ml gin
10 ml Cointreau
2 anchovy-stuffed olives

METHOD
Fill a mixing glass with ice and coat
with vermouth, discarding excess liquid.
Add gin and stir for 10–15 seconds.
Pour Cointreau into a chilled martini
glass and swirl to coat the sides. Discard
remaining liquid. Strain gin into glass
and garnish with olives.

BEIJING FLING
Martini glass

INGREDIENTS
4 peeled chunks of cucumber
50 ml gin
10 ml Lillet
10 ml lemon juice
10 ml sugar syrup
10 ml elderflower cordial
30 ml cloudy apple juice
3 kaffir lime leaves to garnish

METHOD
Muddle cucumber then combine
all ingredients with ice. Shake and
double-strain into a martini glass.
Float the lime leaves on top for effect.

SINGAPORE SLING

Collins glass

INGREDIENTS
30 ml gin
50 ml sour mix
15 ml grenadine
splash of soda water
dash of cherry brandy

METHOD
Fill a shaker with ice, add all
ingredients (except soda water and
brandy). Shake well. Strain into an
ice-filled Collins glass, top with
soda water and float the cherry
brandy on top.

GIN SLING

Martini glass

INGREDIENTS
30 ml gin
20 ml sweet vermouth
15 ml fresh lemon juice
20 ml sugar syrup
dash of Angostura bitters
splash of soda water
lemon peel to garnish

METHOD
Shake all the ingredients (except the
soda water) with ice and strain into a
martini glass. Top with soda water.
Garnish with a spiral of lemon peel.

TOM COLLINS
Highball glass

INGREDIENTS
60 ml gin
45 ml lemon juice
10 ml sugar syrup
splash of soda water

METHOD
Combine gin, juice and sugar syrup
in a highball glass. Stir, add ice and
fill with soda water.

SOUTHERN BELLE
Martini glass

INGREDIENTS
40 ml gin
20 ml Aperol
30 ml lime juice
5 ml sugar syrup
twist of lime to garnish

METHOD
Shake and strain all ingredients
into a martini glass. Garnish with
a twist of lime.

LONDON SUMMER
Tumbler

INGREDIENTS
½ kiwi fruit
½ small lime
pinch of raw sugar
30 ml gin
10 ml black raspberry liqueur

METHOD
Muddle fruit and sugar in a tumbler.
Add ice and crush with other ingredients.

HULA HOOP
Martini glass

INGREDIENTS
**60 ml gin
30 ml orange juice
15 ml pineapple juice
cherry to garnish**

METHOD
Shake all the ingredients with ice and strain into a martini glass. Garnish with a cherry.

CORINTHIAN ICED TEA
Bamboo glass

INGREDIENTS
**45 ml gin
15 ml crème de pomme verte
30 ml white cranberry juice
10 ml lemon juice
10 ml sugar syrup
10 ml cranberry/hibiscus syrup
4 watermelon chunks
8 mint leaves
15 ml rosehip and hibiscus tea
wedge of watermelon to garnish**

METHOD
Combine all ingredients (except tea) in a shaker with ice. Shake and pour into a bamboo glass, then top with tea and crushed ice. Serve with a long straw and garnish with a thin watermelon wedge.

ALICE SPRINGS
Highball glass

INGREDIENTS
60 ml gin
20 ml lemon juice
20 ml orange juice
½ tsp grenadine
3 dashes of Angostura bitters
splash of soda water
½ orange slice to garnish

METHOD
Shake all ingredients (except soda water)
with ice. Pour into a highball glass and
fill with soda. Garnish with orange slice.

SOUTH PAW
Highball glass

INGREDIENTS
30 ml gin
20 ml Campari
splash of sparkling grapefruit juice
2 wedges of fresh lime to garnish

METHOD
Build ingredients in a highball glass
over ice. Garnish with lime wedges.

VIOLENT LITTLE OL' LAVENDER GIRL
Martini glass

INGREDIENTS
6 mint leaves
80 ml lavender-infused gin
10 ml grenadine
10 ml blue curacao
45 ml fresh lychee juice
sprig of lavender to garnish

METHOD
Muddle mint leaves in base of shaker.
Add other ingredients and shake with ice.
Strain and serve in a chilled martini glass.
Garnish with floating lavender sprig.

GIMLET

Martini glass

INGREDIENTS

45 ml gin
10 ml lime juice
wedge of lime to garnish

METHOD

Shake gin and lime juice in a shaker
with ice and strain into a martini glass.
Garnish with a lime wedge.

COLAZIONE

Martini glass

INGREDIENTS

3 chunks of grapefruit
2 tsp raw sugar
40 ml gin
10 ml Campari
20 ml crème de peche
grapefruit peel to garnish

METHOD

Muddle grapefruit with sugar, then
shake with other ingredients and
double-strain into a martini glass.
Garnish with a flamed grapefruit peel.

QUINTINI

Martini glass

INGREDIENTS

50 ml gin
10 ml Lillet
15 ml quince liqueur
dash of orange bitters
shaved orange zest to garnish

METHOD
Shake and strain all ingredients
into a martini glass. Garnish with
orange zest.

MILLER'S MARTINI

Martini glass

INGREDIENTS

60 ml gin
dash of Grand Marnier
dash of orange bitters
mint leaf to garnish

METHOD
Shake and strain all ingredients into a
martini glass. Garnish with a floating
mint leaf.

VANILLA KISS

Martini glass

INGREDIENTS

30 ml gin
15 ml crème de cacao
15 ml butterscotch schnapps
sugar to garnish

METHOD

Shake and double-strain all ingredients
into a chilled martini glass with
sugar-crusted rim.

THE GILBERT
Old-fashioned glass

INGREDIENTS
handful of white grapes
2 slices of ginger
30 ml sloe gin
10 ml crème de gingembre
5 ml black raspberry liqueur
15 ml Jaggard lemon myrtle
5 ml sour mix
grapes to garnish

METHOD
Muddle small handful of grapes
and slices of ginger. Shake with other
ingredients and strain into an
old-fashioned glass. Garnish with
three skewered grapes.

YEMEN FIZZ
Champagne flute

INGREDIENTS
4 red grapes
15 ml gin
10 ml crème de cassis
140 ml Champagne
extra grape to garnish

METHOD
Muddle grapes. Shake all ingredients
and strain into a flute. Top with
Champagne and float a small red grape.

K.G.B.

Martini glass

INGREDIENTS

60 ml gin
30 ml kirsch
30 ml apricot brandy
15 ml lemon juice
1 tsp castor sugar
twist of lemon to garnish

METHOD

Shake all ingredients with ice and strain into a martini glass. Garnish with lemon twist.

TINA'S ON A TAIPEI BUS

Highball glass

INGREDIENTS

30 ml rose petal-infused gin
30 ml vodka
15 ml watermelon liqueur
10 ml crème de gingembre
6 drops of rose water
75 ml pink grapefruit juice
5 ml parfait amour
rose petals to garnish

METHOD

Build all ingredients (except parfait amour) in a highball glass over cubed ice. Stir gently. Float parfait amour over top. Garnish with rose petals.

rum like you stole something

As the signature drop of the tropics, rum can bring out the drunken sailor girl in everyone. Fuelled by mischievous Caribbean libido, this frisky spirit locates the flirt within and teaches us to run with tomfoolery. It conjures sweeping white beaches, tiny polka-dot bikinis and Tiki-decorated shacks with slow-revolving fans. It's a laidback sip that washes away the stress of everyday life, taking us to a tropical stopover, even if just for a moment.

Rum is for the armchair adventurer who sports a pina colada (not milk) moustache and thinks mint leaves are strictly for mojitos (never for cooking). It's for grass-skirted babes who pin flowers in their hair, hold exquisite cocktails and know how to have fun — whether it's under a palm tree or in an urban bar.

The Mai Tai is an old favourite, but to really share the wealth, a good summer punch is in order. Mix up a batch and demand that your friends take part in the escapades, scooping mouthfuls of fruity rum flavours until sunlight ebbs away and the hammock beckons.

FUNKY CARIBBEAN
Martini glass

INGREDIENTS
45 ml vanilla-infused rum
45 ml sauvignon blanc
50 ml pineapple juice
15 ml sugar syrup
vanilla bean to garnish

METHOD
Shake and strain all ingredients into
a chilled martini glass. Garnish with
a split vanilla bean.

CARAMELISED FIG & BANANA DAIQUIRI
Martini glass

INGREDIENTS
40 ml rum
10 ml Licor 43
10 ml butterscotch schnapps
20 ml fig puree
10 ml lemon juice
2 tbsp caramelised banana
caramelised fig to garnish

METHOD
Blend all ingredients with ice and serve
in a martini glass. Add two short straws
and garnish with caramelised fig.

PINA COLADA
Collins glass

INGREDIENTS
90 ml light rum
3 tbsp coconut milk
3 tbsp crushed pineapple

METHOD
Put all ingredients into an electric
blender with two cups of crushed ice.
Blend briefly at a high speed. Strain into
a Collins glass and serve with a straw.

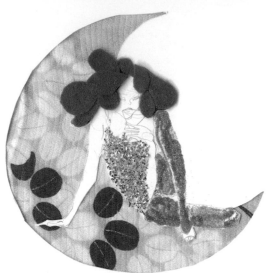

PINK MOON
Martini glass

INGREDIENTS
**40 ml white rum
10 ml Licor 43
5 ml vanilla syrup
½ lime
20 ml pink grapefruit juice
twist of lemon to garnish**

METHOD
Shake ingredients and pour into
a martini glass. Garnish with a
lemon twist.

LAWRENCE ICED T.E.
Bamboo glass

INGREDIENTS
30 ml rum
15 ml cherry liqueur
15 ml peach liqueur
30 ml peach tea
30 ml cranberry juice
15 ml lemon juice
5 ml sugar syrup
30 ml apricot puree
2 thin slices of red chilli to garnish

METHOD
Combine all ingredients with ice then shake and pour into a bamboo glass. Top with crushed ice. Garnish with chilli and serve with a long straw.

ALOHA SCREWDRIVER
Goblet

INGREDIENTS
15 ml coconut-flavoured rum
30 ml vodka
60 ml orange juice
60 ml pineapple juice
2 maraschino cherries to garnish

METHOD
Blend all ingredients with crushed ice until smooth. Pour into a chilled goblet and garnish with maraschino cherries.

STRAWBERRY DAIQUIRI
Martini glass

INGREDIENTS

30 g strawberries
15 ml strawberry schnapps
30 ml light rum
30 ml lime juice
1 tsp castor sugar

METHOD
Muddle strawberries. Shake all
ingredients with ice, strain into
a martini glass, and serve.

ZANZIBAR
Highball glass

INGREDIENTS
3 blueberries
3 strawberries
30 ml vanilla-infused rum
30 ml passionfruit liqueur
2 wedges of lime
90 ml cranberry juice

METHOD
Muddle blueberries and strawberries.
Pour into a highball glass with alcohol
over crushed ice. Add wedges of fresh
lime and finish with cranberry juice.

MOJITO
Highball glass

INGREDIENTS
5 mint leaves
½ cup fresh chopped lime
60 ml white rum
20 ml sugar syrup
3 tsp castor sugar
splash of soda water
sprig of mint to garnish

METHOD
Muddle mint leaves and fresh lime
(with rind). Shake with rum, syrup
and sugar, and pour into a highball
glass. Top with soda water and garnish
with a sprig of mint.

YACHT CLUB PUNCH
Collins glass

INGREDIENTS
30 ml banana-flavoured rum
30 ml whisky
90 ml orange or pineapple juice
splash of soda water
maraschino cherry and slice of
   orange to garnish

METHOD
Fill shaker with ice, add ingredients
(except soda water) and shake well.
Pour into Collins glass and fill with
soda. Garnish with maraschino cherry
and orange slice.

A DAY OFF
Tumbler

INGREDIENTS
1 lime
30 ml Aperol
20 ml dark rum
10 ml lychee liqueur
splash of cloudy apple juice
basil leaf to garnish

METHOD
Slice lime into quarters and mix
with Aperol, rum, liqueur and ice.
Top with apple juice. Garnish with
fresh basil leaf.

RUM RUNNER
Tumbler

INGREDIENTS
60 ml rum
80 ml pineapple juice
30 ml passionfruit juice
**wheel of lime and slice of pineapple
   to garnish**

METHOD
Shake and strain all ingredients
into a tumbler. Garnish with a lime
wheel and pineapple slice.
*For the ultimate Rum Runner, use 30 ml Havana
Club rum (3 year) and 30 ml Havana Club rum
(7 year).*

RUM RELIEF
Highball glass

INGREDIENTS
70 ml rum
90 ml pineapple juice
30 ml orange juice
30 ml coconut liqueur
5 ml overproof rum
wedge of pineapple to garnish

METHOD
Shake and strain all ingredients
(except overproof rum) into a highball
glass. Float overproof rum and garnish
with a pineapple wedge.

RED RUM
Martini glass

INGREDIENTS
30 ml rum
30 ml Cinzano Rosso
10 ml maraschino juice
dash of Angostura bitters
twist of orange to garnish

METHOD
Combine all ingredients, stir and
strain into a chilled martini glass.
Garnish with an orange twist.

TIKI MAI TAI
Hurricane glass

INGREDIENTS
45 ml rum
30 ml hazelnut liqueur
22 ml triple sec
30 ml pineapple juice
30 ml sweet and sour mix

METHOD
Blend all ingredients with 90 g ice
until smooth. Pour into a chilled
hurricane glass.

HURRICANE
Martini glass

INGREDIENTS
30 ml white rum
30 ml dark rum
5 ml passionfruit syrup
15 ml lime juice

METHOD
Shake all ingredients with ice
and strain into a martini glass.

RUM-EO AND JULIET
Collins glass

INGREDIENTS
30 ml light rum
30 ml dark rum
30 ml chocolate-flavoured rum
90 ml cola
1 tbsp 151-proof rum
slice of lemon to garnish

METHOD
Fill a chilled Collins glass with ice and add
light, dark and chocolate rums. Top with
cola and stir gently. Float 151-proof rum.
Garnish with a slice of lemon.

sake in the city

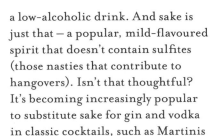

♥

It's an ancient drop (more than 6000 years old, in fact), but the sake trend is finally catching on. These fancy drinks are for women keen to try something different, who like variations on the classics and are ready for a neon-lit Tokyo experience without leaving their bar stools. It's for those wannabe Sofia Coppolas lusting after Lost in Translation moments — where fast-paced living and language barriers confuse the tastebuds and kooky pop culture sits happily alongside geisha grace.

Sake suits the karaoke queen who adores the spotlight but is also ideal for the occasional tippler looking for a low-alcoholic drink. And sake is just that — a popular, mild-flavoured spirit that doesn't contain sulfites (those nasties that contribute to hangovers). Isn't that thoughtful? It's becoming increasingly popular to substitute sake for gin and vodka in classic cocktails, such as Martinis and Cosmopolitans.

Tonight, play the devious hostess and free yourself of predictability. It may be a long way to the top if you want to rock and roll, but it's a mere hop, skip and a jump away from a top night with this Japanese delicacy.

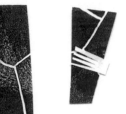

KYOTO PROTOCOL
Martini glass

INGREDIENTS
½ kiwi fruit
⅓ small cucumber
15 ml lime juice
30 ml cloudy apple juice
15 ml sake
30 ml white rum
15 ml crème de pomme verte
10 ml kiwi syrup

METHOD
Muddle kiwi and cucumber. Add juices,
then alcohol. Add ice, shake and
double-strain into a martini glass.

The Cocktail

SAKETINI

Martini glass

INGREDIENTS

dash of dry vermouth
90 ml chilli-infused sake
anchovy-stuffed olive to garnish

METHOD

Wash ice with vermouth and strain thoroughly. Add sake, gently stir and strain into a martini glass. Garnish with anchovy-stuffed olive.

W BAR SAKETINI

Martini glass

INGREDIENTS

30 ml sake
45 ml vodka
15 ml Midori
30 ml lemon juice
10 ml sugar syrup
sugar to garnish

METHOD

Shake and strain all ingredients into a sugar-crusted martini glass.

42 FLYING MULES
Highball glass

INGREDIENTS
½ lime
6 torn mint leaves
½ large thai chilli
30 ml sake
30 ml vodka
10 ml lemon juice
splash of ginger beer
sprig of mint to garnish

METHOD
In a shaker, muddle lime, mint and
chilli. Add sake, vodka, lemon juice and
ice, then shake. Pour into a highball
glass and top with ginger beer. Garnish
with a fresh mint sprig.

The Cocktail

AUTUMN THUNDER
Highball glass

INGREDIENTS

30 ml sake
15 ml black raspberry liqueur
15 ml Cointreau
30 ml orange juice
30 ml pineapple juice
15 ml lime juice
15 ml Benedictine
dash of Angostura bitters
twists of lemon and orange to garnish

METHOD

Place all ingredients in shaker and
mix well. Strain into a highball glass
filled with ice and serve. Garnish with
interlinked orange and lemon twists.

BLOODY MARY
Highball glass

INGREDIENTS

dash of Worcestershire sauce
dash of Tabasco sauce
pinch of wasabi paste
10 ml lemon juice
90 ml tomato juice
45 ml sake
15 ml vodka
celery stalk
freshly cracked black pepper to garnish

METHOD

Pour Worcestershire and Tabasco sauces
into shaker, add wasabi and lemon and
tomato juices. Shake and strain into
a highball glass containing sake, vodka
and celery. Crack pepper on top.

GINGER CHAN
Highball glass

INGREDIENTS

45 ml ginger-infused sake
juice of ½ lime
30 ml apple juice
6 mint leaves
splash of ginger beer

METHOD

Shake sake, juices and mint, then pour
into a highball glass full of ice. Top with
ginger beer.

ANGEL TSUZI
Martini glass

INGREDIENTS

35 ml sake
10 ml orgeat syrup
15 ml Frangelico
30 ml half and half (cream and milk)
ground cinnamon to garnish

METHOD

Combine all ingredients with ice.
Shake and strain into a martini glass.
Garnish with freshly ground cinnamon.

LYCHEE MARTINI
Martini glass

INGREDIENTS
30 ml sherry
150 ml cachaça
15 ml sake
30 ml lychee syrup
5 ml elderflower cordial
stick of lemongrass to garnish

METHOD
Shake and strain all ingredients into
a chilled martini glass. Garnish with
a stick of lemongrass.

GEISHA FIZZ
Champagne flute

INGREDIENTS
2 lychees
10 ml lemon juice
15 ml sake
110 ml Champagne
15 ml crème de gingembre
kaffir lime leaf to garnish

METHOD
Muddle lychees and lemon juice.
Combine all ingredients with ice in
a shaker. Shake and strain into a flute.
Garnish with a broken kaffir lime leaf.

J-POP

Martini glass

INGREDIENTS

3 slices ginger
3 slices nashi pear
45 ml sake
15 ml feijoa vodka
15 ml pear liqueur
10 ml honey
15 ml cloudy apple juice
slice of nashi pear to garnish

METHOD

Muddle ginger and nashi pear.
Combine with other ingredients,
shake and double-strain into a
martini glass. Garnish with a slice
of nashi pear.

JAPANESE PEAR

Martini glass

INGREDIENTS

¼ nashi pear
15 ml sake
45 ml vodka
15 ml apple liqueur
10 ml lemon juice
10 ml pear liqueur
5 g sugar
slice of pear to garnish

METHOD

Muddle nashi pear then combine with
other ingredients. Shake and strain into
a martini glass. Garnish with a pear slice.

the tequila made me do it

If you're up for a big night, then tequila is your not-so-trusty companion. This clear spirit can light you up like a piñata at Carnaval. But friends, beware — one hit too many and a blindfolded demon will take a swing, splitting you clean in two. And before you can cry 'ole!' you'll find yourself on a cold concrete floor somewhere in Mexico City on Constable Pedro's wanted list.

Tequila is for girls who know how to party — it has La Bamba written all over its spirited heart. The Margarita is the most popular use of tequila — it's a flirty one, perfect for loosening tongues, but keep in mind it's a lethal cocktail that goes down smoothly only to knock down the toughest of men.

So put on your best poncho, pin a red rose in your hair and dust on some bronzer. Tonight, señorita, is for making sweet, illicit love — time to be saucy and brazen because, after all, the tequila made you do it …

PASSIONFRUIT MARGARITA

Martini glass

INGREDIENTS
45 ml tequila
15 ml triple sec
30 ml lemon juice
40 ml passionfruit puree
salt to garnish

METHOD
Blend ingredients with ice. Serve in a salt-crusted martini glass.

MANGO MARGARITA

Martini glass

INGREDIENTS
45 ml tequila
15 ml triple sec
15 ml lime juice
15 ml lemon juice
¼ fresh mango
3 sour cherries to garnish

METHOD
Place all ingredients in a blender with ice. Once thick, pour into a martini glass. Garnish with sour cherries.

HOLA MAMASITA
Martini glass

INGREDIENTS
30 ml kaffir lime-infused tequila
15 ml passionfruit liqueur
15 ml crème de gingembre
30 ml passionfruit puree
ground cinnamon to garnish

METHOD
Shake and strain all ingredients into
cinnamon-crusted martini glass.

TEQUILA SUNRISE
Highball glass

INGREDIENTS
45 ml tequila
½ tsp lime juice
splash of orange juice
15 ml grenadine

METHOD
Fill glass with ice; add tequila and lime
juice and stir. Top with orange juice and
trickle grenadine on top.

TEQUILA MOCKINGBIRD
Collins glass

INGREDIENTS
60 ml tequila
30 ml triple sec
90 ml pineapple juice
maraschino cherry to garnish

METHOD
Shake ingredients with ice and strain
into a Collins glass. Garnish with
a maraschino cherry.

TO KILL A ROSE

Martini glass

INGREDIENTS
45 ml raspberry puree
45 ml vanilla cream
15 ml crème de framboise
1 tbs sugar
60 ml rose and berry-infused tequila
dash of rose syrup
rose petals to garnish

METHOD
Heat puree, vanilla cream and crème
de framboise with sugar in a frying pan
for 30 seconds on a high flame. Add
tequila and stir. Pour into a martini
glass, add rose syrup and garnish with
two rose petals.

LOLITA

Martini glass

INGREDIENTS
20 ml tequila
10 ml lime juice
1 tsp honey
2 dashes of Angostura bitters

METHOD
Shake all ingredients and strain into
a martini glass. Serve with a couple
of ice cubes.

MEXICAN ROSE
Tumbler

INGREDIENTS
20 ml tequila
10 ml strawberry schnapps
45 ml milk
15 ml grenadine

METHOD
Shake all ingredients and strain into a tumbler.

MEXICAN MANHATTAN
Martini glass

INGREDIENTS
50 ml tequila
10 ml maraschino juice
10 ml sweet vermouth
2–3 dashes of orange bitters
cherry to garnish

METHOD
Stir all ingredients and serve straight up in a chilled martini glass. Garnish with a cherry (or maraschino when not in season).

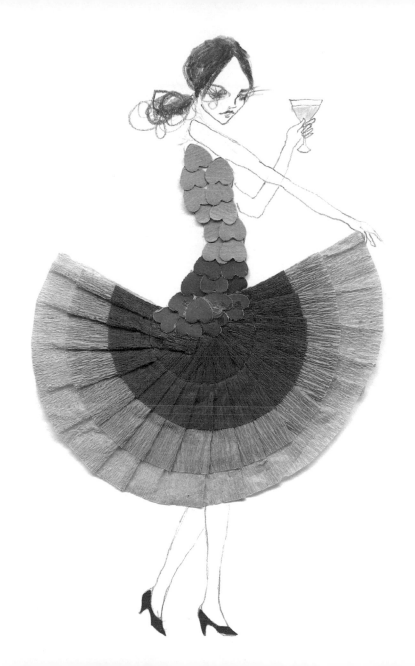

WATERMELON & CORIANDER MARGARITA

Coupette glass

INGREDIENTS

4 chunks of watermelon
10 ml lemon juice
50 ml tequila
10 ml Midori
10 ml coriander syrup
6 coriander leaves
extra coriander leaf to garnish

METHOD

Muddle watermelon and lemon juice.
Then combine all ingredients in a shaker
with ice. Shake and double-strain into
a coupette glass. Float a coriander leaf.

PEPPERED STRAWBERRY MARGARITA

Martini glass

INGREDIENTS

3–4 strawberries
45 ml pepper-infused tequila
20 ml crème de fraise
25 ml lime juice
dash sugar syrup
**cracked pepper and extra strawberry
   to garnish**

METHOD

Muddle strawberries. Add remaining
ingredients, then shake. Serve straight up
in a chilled martini glass. Garnish with
a cracked pepper rim, pepper dusting
and a speared strawberry quarter.

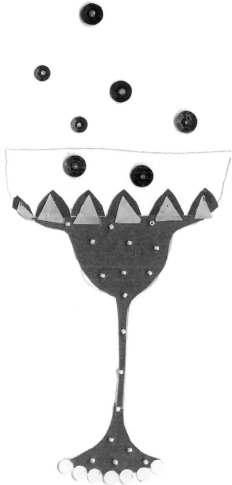

ARABIAN MARGARITA
Coupette glass

INGREDIENTS
45 ml cardamon-infused tequila
15 ml apricot brandy
45 ml apricot puree
15 ml lemon juice
5 ml sugar syrup
dried apricot to garnish

METHOD
Pour all ingredients into a shaker
with ice. Shake and strain into a
coupette glass. Float a dried apricot.

W BAR MARGARITA

Martini glass

INGREDIENTS
45 ml pepper-infused tequila
15 ml triple sec
25 ml lime juice
dash of sugar syrup
cracked pepper to garnish

METHOD
Shake all ingredients and serve
straight up in a martini glass.
Garnish with a cracked pepper rim
and a pepper dusting.

LIME STREET MARGARITA

Coupette glass

INGREDIENTS
½ mandarine, peeled
10 ml lime juice
10 ml lemon juice
45 ml tequila
15 ml mandarine liqueur
10 ml sugar syrup
4 raspberries
salt to garnish

METHOD
Muddle mandarine with lime and
lemon juices. Combine all ingredients
with ice, shake and strain into a half
salt-encrusted coupette glass.

BLUE MARGARITA

Martini glass

INGREDIENTS

45 ml tequila
15 ml Grand Marnier
30 ml blue curacao
30 ml lime juice
dash of sugar syrup
salt to garnish

METHOD

Shake all ingredients with ice.
Strain into a salt-crusted martini glass.

HIMALAYA
Martini glass

INGREDIENTS
⅓ nashi pear
10 ml lemon juice
30 ml tequila
20 ml chamomile liqueur
10 ml green apple liqueur
5 ml caramel liqueur
5 ml cinnamon syrup
slice of nashi pear to garnish

METHOD
Muddle nashi and lemon juice in a
mixing glass. Combine with other
ingredients and ice and shake.
Double-strain into a martini glass.
Garnish with a slice of nashi pear.

The Cocktail

SCIMITAR
Martini glass

INGREDIENTS
30 ml tequila
30 ml Licor 43
30 ml espresso
kiwi slice to garnish

METHOD
Pour all ingredients into a mixing glass with ice. Shake and double-strain into a martini glass. Garnish with a kiwi slice skewer.

EL STAMOSA
Martini glass

INGREDIENTS
¼ green apple
¼ fresh peach
3 wedges of lime
10 ml peach puree
40 ml kaffir lime-infused tequila
10 ml green apple liqueur
15 ml Nothing liqueur
45 ml apple juice
5 ml sugar syrup
kaffir lime leaf to garnish

METHOD
Muddle fruit. Combine with remaining ingredients, then shake and serve straight up in a chilled martini glass. Garnish with a floated kaffir lime leaf.

vodka vixens

❣

Depending on how and with whom you consume it, vodka can either be your one-way ticket to an Orwellian down-and-out-in-London experience, or make you feel like a Manhattanite flirting in the East Village all night long. It's an elegant drop, now infused with all manner of fruit to keep us guessing, but let it be known that vodka is for women who take risks — women who tease and conquer and command the attention of dangerous men.

Vodka is as racy as a Bond girl, as alluring as a 50s Hollywood starlet and as compelling as a KGB agent dabbling in a little Russian roulette. Most importantly, vodka is versatile, adopting the flavour of whatever you choose to mix it with — it can seduce in the form of a Vodkatini or ease the pain as a Bloody Mary. It even captured the hearts of viewers worldwide as the cashed-up girls from Sex and the City downed Cosmopolitans aplenty.

Far from passé, vodka cocktails are part of the establishment when it comes to serious drinking. It's for every woman, from the peroxide blonde, wannabe rocker hanging around bars to glimpse her favourite rock star to the couture princess who allures in less amplified ways.

W BAR MARTINI

Martini glass

INGREDIENTS
40 ml vodka
10 ml black raspberry liqueur
10 ml absinth
dash of cranberry juice
dash of lemon juice
dash of sugar syrup
cranberries and twist of lemon
   to garnish

METHOD
Shake all ingredients and strain into
a chilled martini glass. Garnish with
speared cranberries and a lemon twist.

CRANAPPLE MARTINI

Martini glass

INGREDIENTS
30 ml citrus-infused vodka
30 ml Cointreau
dash of crème de gingembre
30 ml cranberry juice
30 ml apple juice
15 ml fresh lime juice
splash of ginger beer
squeeze of lime and ginger slice
   to garnish

METHOD
Shake all ingredients and strain into
a chilled martini glass. Garnish with a
lime squeeze and a speared ginger slice.

STILETTO MARTINI
Martini glass

INGREDIENTS
5 chunks of pineapple
sliver of ginger
4 coriander leaves
60 ml pineapple-infused vodka
20 ml clear apple juice
2 tsp almond syrup

METHOD
Muddle pineapple, ginger and coriander
leaves. Combine with vodka, apple juice
and almond syrup. Double-strain into a
martini glass and serve.

PEAR & GINGER FIZZ
Champagne flute

INGREDIENTS
30 ml vodka
10 ml crème de gingembre
30 ml pear puree
splash of Champagne
slice of pear to garnish

METHOD
Shake and strain vodka, crème de
gingembre and puree into a flute and
top with Champagne. Garnish with
a pear slice.

GINGER & LEMONGRASS MARTINI
Martini glass

INGREDIENTS
60 ml vodka
10 ml sugar syrup
1 cm slice of fresh lemongrass root
fine slice of ginger
strip of lemongrass to garnish

METHOD
Muddle lemongrass and ginger.
Shake with vodka and sugar syrup and
double-strain into a martini glass.
Garnish with a lemongrass strip.

APPLE & CORIANDER MARTINI
Martini glass

INGREDIENTS
½ Granny Smith apple
5 coriander leaves
40 ml vodka
20 ml crème de pomme verte
15 ml clear apple juice
dash of lime juice
extra coriander leaf to garnish

METHOD
Muddle apple and coriander.
Combine with alcohol. Shake and
strain into a martini glass. Float a
coriander leaf on top.

SEABREEZE

Highball glass

INGREDIENTS

45 ml vodka
120 ml cranberry juice
30 ml grapefruit juice
wedge of lime to garnish

METHOD
Pour vodka and juice into a highball glass with ice and stir well. Garnish with a lime wedge.

CLASSIC BLOODY MARY

Highball glass

INGREDIENTS

60 ml vodka
90 ml tomato juice
15 ml lemon juice
black pepper and salt
3 dashes of Worcestershire sauce
2 drops of Tabasco sauce
wedge of lemon and celery stick
  to garnish

METHOD
Shake all ingredients with ice and strain into a highball glass over crushed ice. Garnish with a lemon wedge and celery stick.

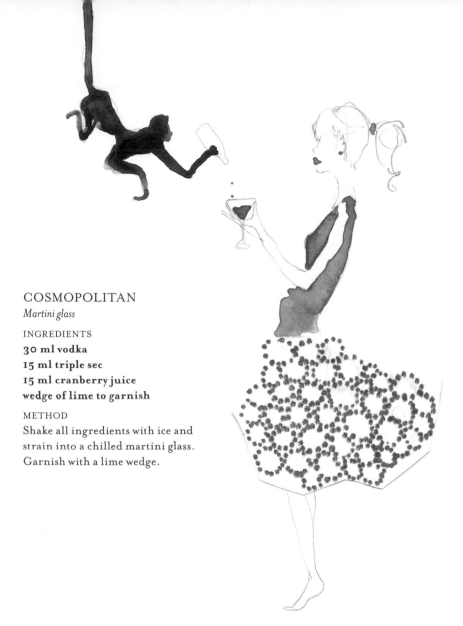

COSMOPOLITAN
Martini glass

INGREDIENTS
30 ml vodka
15 ml triple sec
15 ml cranberry juice
wedge of lime to garnish

METHOD
Shake all ingredients with ice and
strain into a chilled martini glass.
Garnish with a lime wedge.

EASTERN BREAKFAST MARTINI
Martini glass

INGREDIENTS

30 ml citrus-infused vodka
15 ml quince liqueur
15 ml Cointreau
2 drops of orange bitters
10 ml lemon juice
1 tbsp quince jam
twist of orange to garnish

METHOD

Shake all ingredients with ice and
strain into a martini glass. Garnish
with a twist of orange.

BAGHDAD ICED TEA
Bamboo glass

INGREDIENTS
¼ green apple
6 mint leaves
30 ml apple juice
15 ml lime juice
40 ml vodka
15 ml apple liqueur
5 ml gin
10 ml rose syrup
15 ml jasmine tea
2 slices of red chilli to garnish

METHOD
Muddle apple, mint leaves, apple juice and lime juice. Shake with vodka, liqueur, gin, rose syrup and ice, and pour into a bamboo glass. Top with tea and crushed ice. Garnish with chilli slices and serve with a long straw.

LONG ISLAND ICED TEA
Highball glass

INGREDIENTS
30 ml vodka
30 ml gin
30 ml light rum
30 ml tequila
30 ml lemon juice
30 ml orange liqueur
1 tsp castor sugar
90 ml cola
slice of lemon and lime to garnish

METHOD
Pour all ingredients into a highball glass full of ice and stir. Garnish with half a slice of lemon and half a slice of lime, and serve with a swizzle stick and two tall straws.

HIBISCUS MARTINI
Martini glass

INGREDIENTS
45 ml vodka
15 ml blackberry liqueur
20 ml cranberry juice
20 ml apple juice
10 ml hibiscus cordial
dash of lemon juice
cranberry to garnish

METHOD
Shake all ingredients and strain
into a martini glass. Garnish with
a speared cranberry.

HAWAIIAN PIMMS
Pilsner glass

INGREDIENTS
½ lemon, cut into wedges
5 mint leaves
5 ml sugar syrup
40 ml Pimms
20 ml vodka
splash of ginger beer

METHOD
Muddle lemon, mint and sugar.
Combine with ice, Pimms and vodka,
and shake. Serve in a Pilsner glass and
top with ginger beer.

ORANGE & PEACH SWIZZLE
Martini glass

INGREDIENTS
30 ml vodka
15 ml peach liqueur
20 ml lemon juice
30 ml passionfruit puree
3–4 dashes of orange bitters
slice of peach, vanilla sugar and
    passionfruit pulp to garnish

METHOD
Shake all ingredients and serve straight
up in a chilled martini glass. Garnish
with a speared peach slice and a pinch
of vanilla sugar and drizzle passionfruit
pulp at the bottom of the glass.

VELVET UNDERGROUND
Martini glass

INGREDIENTS
45 ml honey-infused vodka
15 ml apple liqueur
45 ml apple puree
10 ml lemon juice
2 drops of balsamic vinegar
slice of apple to garnish

METHOD
Shake vodka, liqueur, puree and juice
with ice, then double-strain into a
martini glass. Drop balsamic vinegar in
the centre of the glass and garnish with a
round slice of apple.

VANILLA PASSION
Martini glass

INGREDIENTS
45 ml vanilla-infused vodka
15 ml apple juice
30 ml passionfruit puree
15 ml caramel liqueur
2–3 dashes of lime
splash of vanilla sugar syrup
passionfruit pulp and vanilla bean
to garnish

METHOD
Shake all ingredients and serve
straight up in a chilled martini glass.
Garnish with passionfruit pulp and
a split vanilla bean.

BERRY SLUSH
Martini glass

INGREDIENTS
15 ml vodka
15 ml black raspberry liqueur
15 ml crème de fraise des bois
15 ml triple sec
30 ml sour mix
60 ml mixed berry puree

METHOD
Place all ingredients in a blender
with ice. Serve in a martini glass.

BLOOD ORANGE BITTER HAND

Martini glass

INGREDIENTS

45 ml vodka
15 ml Cointreau
30 ml blood orange juice
dash of orange bitters
orange zest to garnish

METHOD

Shake and strain all ingredients into a martini glass. Garnish with flamed orange zest.

BUSH TUCKERMAN'S SINUS CLEANER

Martini glass

INGREDIENTS

30 ml tamarind-infused vodka
15 ml vodka
15 ml Jaggard lemon myrtle
10 ml honey liqueur
15 ml lemon juice
10 ml sweet ginger concentrate
30 ml mineral water
5 ml honey
wheel of lemon to garnish

METHOD

Shake all ingredients with ice and strain into a chilled martini glass. Garnish with a lemon wheel.

BASIL BOO
Martini glass

INGREDIENTS
6 fresh basil leaves
2 wedges of lime
10 ml coconut syrup
30 ml orange-infused vodka
30 ml pineapple-infused vodka
30 ml fresh pineapple pulp
30 ml pineapple juice

METHOD
Muddle basil, lime and coconut syrup.
Shake with other ingredients and ice,
and strain into a martini glass.

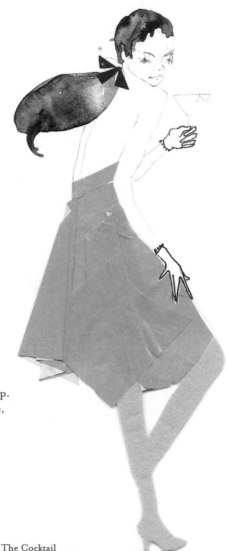

CITRUS LIME GIMLET

Martini glass

INGREDIENTS
90 ml citrus-infused vodka
40 ml lime juice
40 ml sugar syrup
wheel of lime to garnish

METHOD
Shake all ingredients with ice
and strain into a martini glass.
Garnish with a lime wheel.

ELDERTINI

Martini glass

INGREDIENTS
50 ml vodka
10 ml Cinzano Bianco
15 ml orange elderflower cordial
twist of lemon to garnish

METHOD
Shake and strain all ingredients
into a martini glass. Garnish with
a lemon twist.

RED DEATH
Old-fashioned glass

INGREDIENTS
30 ml vodka
30 ml Southern Comfort
30 ml amaretto
15 ml sloe gin
15 ml triple sec
dash of lime juice
splash of orange juice

METHOD
Pour all ingredients (except orange juice) over ice in an old-fashioned glass. Fill with orange juice.

KRACKED
Highball glass

INGREDIENTS
2 strawberries
10 ml lemon juice
40 ml vanilla-infused vodka
10 ml crème de cassis
10 ml crème de fraise
30 ml red fruits tea
cracked pepper to garnish

METHOD
Muddle strawberries and lemon juice. Shake with remaining ingredients and ice, and strain into a highball glass over ice cubes. Open the strainer to release some fruit for texture, then top with crushed ice. Garnish with cracked pepper and serve with a long straw.

PAUL'S POISON
Martini glass

INGREDIENTS
30 ml vanilla-infused vodka
30 ml lemon juice
30 ml apple liqueur
dash of sugar syrup
cherry to garnish

METHOD
Shake all ingredients and pour into a
martini glass. Garnish with a cherry.

SCREWDRIVER
Highball glass

INGREDIENTS
45 ml vodka
60 ml orange juice
slice of orange to garnish

METHOD
Pour vodka and orange juice over ice in a highball glass. Cut orange slice in half and sit both pieces on the rim of the glass.

KAMIKAZE
Tumbler

INGREDIENTS
30 ml vodka
30 ml triple sec
30 ml lime juice

METHOD
Shake ingredients with ice and strain into a tumbler.

CHI-CHI
Wine glass

INGREDIENTS
45 ml vodka
120 ml pineapple juice
30 ml coconut cream
slice of pineapple and cherry to garnish

METHOD
Mix vodka, pineapple juice and coconut
cream with a cup of ice in an electric
blender on high. Pour into a wine glass
and garnish with a pineapple slice
and cherry.

The Cocktail

SEX ON THE BEACH
Highball glass

INGREDIENTS
30 ml vodka
20 ml peach schnapps
60 ml cranberry juice
60 ml grapefruit juice
wedge of lime to garnish

METHOD
Shake all the ingredients with ice
and strain into a highball glass.
Garnish with a lime wedge.

WHITE RUSSIAN
Old-fashioned glass

INGREDIENTS
30 ml vodka
30 ml light cream
30 ml Kahlúa

METHOD
Shake all the ingredients with ice and strain into an old-fashioned glass over ice cubes.

CONFUCIUS
Martini glass

INGREDIENTS
6 longans
4 chunks of fresh ginger
15 ml fresh lemon juice
5 ml longan syrup
45 ml lemongrass-infused vodka
15 ml sake
extra longan to garnish

METHOD
Muddle longans with ginger. Add juice, syrup and alcohol. Shake on ice and double-strain into a martini glass. Garnish with a skewered longan.

GODMOTHER
Highball glass

INGREDIENTS
60 ml vodka
30 ml amaretto

METHOD
Stir both ingredients in a mixing glass
with ice and strain into a highball glass.

RETROINFUSION
Martini glass

INGREDIENTS
30 ml strawberry-infused vodka
30 ml vanilla-infused vodka
30 ml passionfruit liqueur
1 passionfruit

METHOD
Shake alcohol with ice and strain into
a chilled martini glass. Pour pulp of
whole passionfruit over the top and stir.

MOULIN ROUGE

Tumbler

INGREDIENTS
10 raspberries
1 lemon
30 ml honey-infused vodka
15 ml black raspberry liqueur
15 ml macadamia nut liqueur
mint leaf to garnish

METHOD
Muddle fresh raspberries and lemon.
Combine with alcohol, shake and serve
with crushed ice. Garnish with mint.

FARRANG

Tumbler

INGREDIENTS
½ lime
1 tsp sugar
5 coriander leaves
30 ml chilli-infused vodka
15 ml crème de gingembre

METHOD
Muddle lime, sugar and coriander and
combine with crushed ice in a tumbler.
Top with vodka and crème de gingembre.
Stir and serve.

ROSE & ORANGE BLOSSOM MARTINI
Martini glass

INGREDIENTS
40 ml rose petal-infused vodka
15 ml Cointreau
5 ml Campari
30 ml pink grapefruit juice
3 drops of orange bitters
10 ml sugar syrup
orange zest to garnish

METHOD
Pour all ingredients into a mixing glass
with ice. Shake and double-strain into
a martini glass. Garnish with burnt
orange zest.

CITRUS FINISH
Martini glass

INGREDIENTS
45 ml citrus-infused vodka
30 ml Cointreau
splash of Champagne
1 lemon
twist of lemon and orange to garnish

METHOD
Shake vodka and Cointreau and strain
into a martini glass. Top with Champagne
and a squeeze of lemon. Garnish with
twists of lemon and orange.

CAMPRINHA
Highball glass

INGREDIENTS
1 lime, cut into wedges
1 tsp sugar
15 ml vodka
30 ml Campari
15 ml lime liqueur
wedge of lemon to garnish

METHOD
Muddle lime and sugar. Combine with alcohol and serve on ice. Garnish with a lemon wedge.

CAIPIROSKA
Tumbler

INGREDIENTS
2 limes, cut into wedges
½ tsp sugar
60 ml vodka

METHOD
Muddle lime and sugar at the bottom of a tumbler. Cover with crushed ice and top with vodka.

VALENTINE

Martini glass

INGREDIENTS

50 ml flower-infused vodka
10 ml black raspberry liqueur
pomegranate molasses to garnish

METHOD

Pour vodka and liqueur into a blender.
Mix well and serve immediately in a
molasses-rimmed martini glass.

MISTY BITCH

Highball glass

INGREDIENTS

30 ml vodka
30 ml Campari
1 lime
splash of pink grapefruit juice

METHOD

Mix vodka and Campari in a highball
glass. Add fresh lime to taste and top
with pink grapefruit juice.

CHOCOLATE MARTINI
Martini glass

INGREDIENTS
3 chocolate drops
cocoa to garnish
30 ml vodka
30 ml white crème de cacao

METHOD
Place chocolate drops in the bottom of
a martini glass and dust rim with cocoa.
Shake vodka and crème de cacao with
ice, and strain into a martini glass.

PURPLE HAZE

Champagne flute

INGREDIENTS
3 lychees
5 ml lemon juice
15 ml white grapefruit juice
45 ml vodka
10 ml basil syrup
5 ml elderflower cordial
purple basil leaf to garnish

METHOD
Muddle lychees, lemon juice and
grapefruit juice, then add remaining
ingredients and ice. Shake and double-
strain into a flute. Float a purple basil
leaf to garnish.

HAPPY MEDIUM

Martini glass

INGREDIENTS
25 ml spiced rum
25 ml chocolate-infused vodka
5 ml cinnamon syrup
cinnamon stick to garnish

METHOD
Stir all ingredients and serve in a martini
glass. Garnish with a cinnamon stick.

APHRODITE

Martini glass

INGREDIENTS

30 ml orange-infused vodka
50 ml peach-infused vodka
30 ml grenadine
30 ml lemon juice
30 ml raspberry puree

METHOD
Shake all ingredients with ice,
and strain into a martini glass.

AFTER SEX

Collins glass

INGREDIENTS

20 ml vodka
10 ml crème de banane
splash of orange juice

METHOD
Pour vodka and crème de banane
over ice in a Collins glass and fill
with orange juice.

KINKY COSMO
Martini glass

INGREDIENTS
30 ml citrus-infused vodka
30 ml black raspberry liqueur
40 ml pink grapefruit juice
10 ml fresh lime juice
twist of orange to garnish

METHOD
Shake and strain all ingredients into
a martini glass. Garnish with a twist
of orange.

MARTINI ESPRESSO
Martini glass

INGREDIENTS
45 ml coffee bean-infused vodka
15 ml Frangelico
15 ml Kahlúa

METHOD
Shake all ingredients with ice and
strain into a chilled martini glass.

HONEY ESPRESSO
Martini glass

INGREDIENTS
30 ml vodka
30 ml honey-infused vodka
5 ml sugar syrup
30 ml espresso shot
coffee beans to garnish

METHOD
Shake all ingredients and double-strain
into a martini glass. Garnish with three
coffee beans.

MUDSLIDE
Highball glass

INGREDIENTS
60 ml vodka
60 ml Kahlúa
60 ml Irish cream

METHOD
Shake all ingredients with crushed ice.
Serve in a chilled highball glass.

HEAD CLEANER

Martini glass

INGREDIENTS

40 ml vodka
30 ml lemon juice
10 ml ginger wine
dash of sugar syrup
crystallised ginger to garnish

METHOD
Shake all ingredients and pour into
a martini glass. Garnish with a piece
of crystallised ginger.

TIBETAN MULE

Highball glass

INGREDIENTS

4 chunks of pineapple
5 coriander stalks
10 ml lime juice
30 ml pineapple-infused vodka
15 ml sake
15 ml crème de gingembre
10 ml coriander syrup
45 ml ginger beer
coriander leaf to garnish

METHOD
Muddle pineapple, coriander stalks and
lime juice. Combine with vodka, sake,
crème de gingembre, coriander syrup
and ice, and shake. Pour into a highball
glass, opening the strainer to release some
fruit for texture, and top with ginger beer.
Garnish with a coriander leaf.

TERRA FIRMA
Martini glass

INGREDIENTS
45 ml feijoa-infused vodka
30 ml crème de gingembre
15 ml Lark's Bush Liqueur
15 ml elderberry flower syrup
dash of Angostura bitters
slice of ginger to garnish

METHOD
Shake vodka, liqueurs and elderberry
and pour into a martini glass. Add a
dash of bitters and garnish with fresh
ginger skewered on a toothpick.

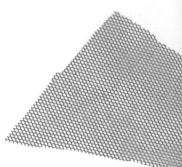

going against the grain

Whisky and its white trash cousin, bourbon, are no longer just a guy's best friend. There are plenty of modern women who don't mind the hearty drop, and the rush of grainy cocktails being served in bars is 100% distilled proof.

There's an outlaw's bravado associated with bourbon. It's biker tough and — like old-school bikers — it sometimes smells as if it hasn't bathed in months. But before you write off bourbon or whisky as being too low-frill or groupie for your Jimmy Choo shoes, take a swig and reappraise.

These drinks are primal and, honey, they're not low carb. They're Real Drinks for Real Babes who think that Atkins died because he didn't have enough bourbon in his diet. For a classic drop, try the Manhattan or Rusty Nail. For something edgy and new, chirp like a Kentucky Bluebird or dig your heels in with a Stiletto. These dark drops are for devoted dames who don't give a damn, Miss Scarlett.

BRITISH RAJ

Old-fashioned glass

INGREDIENTS

¼ pear
60 ml single malt whisky
20 ml star anise sugar syrup
30 ml lime juice
slices of pear and lime to garnish

METHOD

Muddle pear, then shake with whisky, syrup and juice. Strain into an old-fashioned glass over crushed ice. Garnish with a slice of pear and lime.

GENTLEMAN'S AGREEMENT

Martini glass

INGREDIENTS

60 ml bourbon
20 ml Grand Marnier
10 ml caramel syrup
raisins to garnish

METHOD

Pour ingredients into a martini glass, stir and serve. Garnish with raisins steeped in bourbon.

KENTUCKY BLUEBIRD
Martini glass

INGREDIENTS
8 blueberries
10 ml caramel syrup
30 ml bourbon
10 ml barrel-proof bourbon
15 ml blueberry liqueur
15 ml vanilla liqueur
10 ml cabernet sauvignon
10 ml lemon juice
20 ml cloudy apple juice
4 blueberries to garnish

METHOD
Muddle blueberries and caramel syrup.
Combine with other ingredients and ice,
then shake and strain into a chilled martini
glass. Garnish with four blueberries, either
on a skewer or floating across the top.

WHISKY DATE SOUR
Old-fashioned glass

INGREDIENTS
45 ml date-infused whisky
45 ml lemon juice
10 ml egg white
dash of Angostura bitters

METHOD
Shake all ingredients and strain into
an old-fashioned glass.

WHISKY MULE
Highball glass

INGREDIENTS
60 ml whisky
30 ml lime juice
10 ml sugar syrup
splash of ginger beer
sprig of mint to garnish

METHOD
Shake and strain whisky, juice and syrup
into a highball glass. Top with ginger
beer and garnish with a mint sprig.

MS FANNY U BANK
Old-fashioned glass

INGREDIENTS
60 ml bourbon
15 ml mandarine liqueur
30 ml lemon juice
15 ml maple syrup
dash of egg white
slices of mandarine to garnish

METHOD
Shake bourbon, liqueur, juice and syrup
with a dash of egg white, and pour over
crushed ice into old-fashioned glass.
Garnish with mandarine slices.

STILETTO

Old-fashioned glass

INGREDIENTS

45 ml bourbon
1½ tsp amaretto
juice of ½ lemon

METHOD

Pour all ingredients into an
old-fashioned glass over ice and stir.

RUSTY NAIL

Old-fashioned glass

INGREDIENTS

30 ml whisky
40 ml Drambuie

METHOD

Pour whisky and Drambuie into an
old-fashioned glass, with ice.

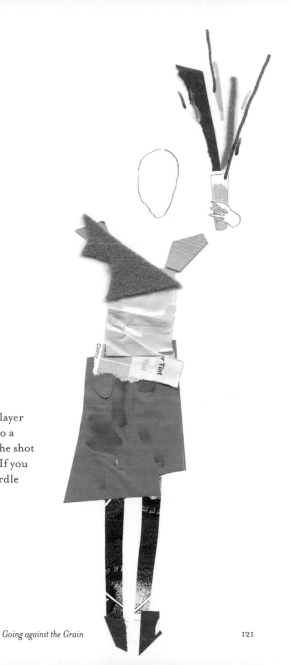

IRISH CAR BOMB

Pilsner glass/Shot glass

INGREDIENTS

15 ml Baileys Irish Cream
15 ml whisky
400 ml Guinness Stout

METHOD

Pour Baileys into a shot glass and layer
whisky on top. Pour Guinness into a
Pilsner glass and let settle. Drop the shot
glass into the Guinness and chug. If you
don't drink this quickly, it will curdle
and taste horrible.

HIGHLAND BREEZE

Highball glass

INGREDIENTS

45 ml whisky
60 ml cranberry juice
splash of pink grapefruit juice
slice of lime to garnish

METHOD

Pour ingredients into a highball
glass with ice. Garnish with lime.

The Cocktail

SIT BACK AND RELAX
Highball glass

INGREDIENTS
3–4 slices of lime
4–5 mint leaves
1 tsp brown sugar
60 ml whisky
15 ml Grand Marnier
sprig of mint to garnish

METHOD
Muddle limes, mint and sugar at the
base of a highball glass. Build whisky
and Grand Marnier on top. Garnish
with a mint sprig.

BOURBON STONE MARTINI
Martini glass

INGREDIENTS
45 ml bourbon
30 ml orange curacao
30 ml fresh lemon juice
30 ml orange juice
1 tsp castor sugar

METHOD
Shake all ingredients with ice and
strain into a martini glass.

MANHATTAN
Martini glass

INGREDIENTS

75 ml bourbon
20 ml sweet vermouth
4 dashes of Angostura bitters
maraschino cherry
orange peel to garnish

METHOD

Combine bourbon, vermouth and bitters in a mixing glass with ice. Strain over a cherry placed in a chilled martini glass. Rub the cut edge of the orange peel over the glass rim and twist it over the drink.

PAUL'S MANHATTAN
Highball glass

INGREDIENTS

75 ml whisky
10 ml Dubbonet Red
10 ml extra-dry vermouth
dash of Angostura bitters
2 tsp of maraschino juice
cherry and twist of lemon to garnish

METHOD

Combine all ingredients and stir well. Strain over ice in a highball glass. Garnish with a cherry and lemon twist.

OLD-FASHIONED
WHISKY SOUR
Martini glass

INGREDIENTS
45 ml whisky
2 dashes of Angostura bitters
1 tbsp cherry juice
150 ml sweet and sour mix
olives or mushrooms to garnish

METHOD
Mix whisky, bitters and cherry juice in
an ice-filled martini glass, and fill the
remainder of the glass with sour mix.
Garnish with olives or mushrooms and
serve with a swizzle stick.

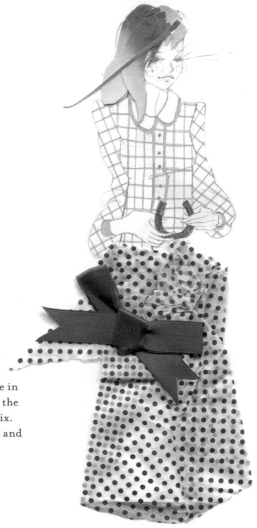

OLD FASHIONED

Old-fashioned glass

INGREDIENTS

1 tsp sugar
splash of water
2 dashes of Angostura bitters
1 maraschino cherry
wedge of orange
60 ml bourbon

METHOD

Mix sugar, water and bitters in an
old-fashioned glass. Add cherry and
orange wedge. Muddle into a paste,
then add bourbon. Fill with ice and stir.

BOURBON MILK PUNCH

Old-fashioned glass

INGREDIENTS

60 ml bourbon
90 ml half and half (cream and milk)
1 tsp castor sugar
¼ tsp vanilla extract
¼ tsp grated nutmeg to garnish

METHOD

Shake all the ingredients with ice cubes
and strain into an old-fashioned glass.
Garnish with nutmeg on top.

GODFATHER

Old-fashioned glass

INGREDIENTS

30 ml bourbon

30 ml amaretto

2 wedges of lime to garnish

METHOD

Build bourbon and amaretto in
an ice-filled old-fashioned glass.
Top with lime wedges.

BOURBON COLLINS

Collins glass

INGREDIENTS

60 ml bourbon

30 ml fresh lemon juice

30 ml sugar syrup

splash of soda water

cherry and slice of orange to garnish

METHOD

Fill two-thirds of a Collins glass
with ice, and pour ingredients over it.
Garnish with a cherry and a slice
of orange.

BOSTON SOUR
Whisky sour glass

INGREDIENTS
60 ml whisky
juice of ½ lemon
1 tsp castor sugar
1 egg white
2 dashes of Angostura bitters
slice of lemon
cherry to garnish

METHOD
Shake whisky, lemon juice, sugar and
egg white with ice and slice of lemon
into a whisky sour glass, top with the
cherry, and serve.

MINT JULEP
Old-fashioned glass

INGREDIENTS
I tsp castor sugar
5–6 mint leaves
90 ml bourbon
sprig of mint to garnish

METHOD
Muddle mint leaves with castor sugar and a splash of water in an old-fashioned glass. Fill with ice, top with bourbon and garnish with mint sprig.

AMERICAN SWEETHEART
Tumbler

INGREDIENTS
30 ml bourbon
30 ml Southern Comfort
dash of dry vermouth
splash of sweet and sour mix

METHOD
Shake all ingredients with ice,
and pour into a tumbler.

SOUTHERN SHAG

Highball glass

INGREDIENTS

45 ml Southern Comfort
60 ml cranberry juice
15 ml orange juice
wedge of lime to garnish

METHOD

Fill a highball glass with ice, add
Southern Comfort and cranberry
and orange juices, then stir.
Garnish with a lime wedge.

SWIZZLE

Highball glass

INGREDIENTS

5 chunks of pineapple
½ orange, peeled and quartered
1 tsp vanilla sugar
4 dashes of Angostura bitters
50 ml bourbon
10 ml lemon juice
dash of Grand Marnier
sprig of mint to garnish

METHOD

Muddle fruit, sugar and bitters.
Add bourbon. Fill ½ a highball glass
with crushed ice. Stir and top with
fresh ice. Float Grand Marnier on
top and garnish with a mint sprig.

LOUISVILLE COOLER
Old-fashioned glass

INGREDIENTS
60 ml bourbon
30 ml orange juice
15 ml lime juice
I tsp castor sugar
slice of orange to garnish

METHOD
Shake all ingredients with ice cubes and
strain into an old-fashioned glass over
ice. Garnish with an orange slice.

ALABAMA SLAMMER

Highball glass

INGREDIENTS

30 ml Southern Comfort
15 ml sloe gin
15 ml amaretto
splash of orange juice
slice of orange to garnish

METHOD

Fill a highball glass with ice, add
ingredients and stir. Garnish with
orange slice.

SOCRATES

Martini glass

INGREDIENTS

60 ml whisky
30 ml apricot brandy
1 tsp triple sec
dash of Angostura bitters

METHOD

Combine all ingredients in a mixing
glass with ice, stir and strain into a
martini glass.

for the mixed-up gal

❣

We've all been lost and jaded in life, walked the path less followed and failed in our attempts. We knew the path we chose meant trouble, but we went along for the ride anyway. It's on nights like these that you need to take a leaf out of this chapter. Round up your drinking buddies to sweep up the mess (by getting mischievously messy all over again).

The mixed-up gal is a unique fashionista — she mixes the new with a touch of the vintage, teams faux pas stoles with well-worn jeans, pleated skirts with fishnet stockings and fitted boots, ruffled shirts with a tight second-hand sweater. She doesn't follow fashion rules dictated by the glossies — she's a find in her own right and takes the best of what she stumbles across.

This chapter is for girls who can't decide on a signature drink, but want to get the best of all worlds. When you do slip up, consider a Freudian Slip or, for something more cheeky, there's Beneath The Sheets for some hotted-up fun. Whatever your plight in life, the mixed-up gal is sure to keep things interesting (to say the least).

KENTUCKY APPLE
Highball glass

INGREDIENTS
2–3 chunks of apple
15 ml elderflower cordial
45 ml bourbon
15 ml green apple liqueur
45 ml apple juice
wedge of apple to garnish

METHOD
Muddle apple and elderflower cordial.
Shake with remaining ingredients.
Strain over ice – ½ cubed, ½ crushed
– into a highball glass. Garnish with a
speared apple wedge.

SPRITZER
Highball glass

INGREDIENTS
90 ml white wine
60 ml soda water
slice of lemon or orange to garnish

METHOD
Fill a highball glass with ice, then fill
three-quarters with wine and the
remainder with soda water. Garnish
with a twist of lemon or orange.

KARMA SIP TRA
Old-fashioned glass

INGREDIENTS
2 lime chunks
6 seedless red grapes
6 mint leaves
30 ml Bacardi Limon
20 ml Cinzano Bianco
10 ml blackberry liqueur
30 ml apple juice
dash of soda water
sprig of mint to garnish

METHOD
Muddle fruit with mint. Combine with
alcohol, juice and ice. Shake and pour
into an old-fashioned glass. Top with
soda water and crushed ice. Garnish with
a sprig of mint.

OPIUM
Old-fashioned glass

INGREDIENTS
10 blueberries
6 blackberries
2 strawberries
15 ml sugar syrup
4 mint leaves
30 ml white rum
15 ml Jaggard lemon myrtle
15 ml black raspberry liqueur
10 ml crème de gingembre
45 ml cranberry juice
ginger to garnish

METHOD
Muddle fruit, sugar syrup and mint,
and shake with other ingredients into
a rocks glass. Garnish with finely
chopped ginger.

GRASSHOPPER
Martini glass

INGREDIENTS
30 ml crème de menthe
30 ml white crème de cacao
30 ml light cream

METHOD
Shake all ingredients with ice.
Strain into a martini glass and serve.

YANG TAO
Martini glass

INGREDIENTS
½ kiwi fruit
30 ml Cointreau
15 ml crème de fraise
15 ml white rum
30 ml guava juice
strawberry to garnish

METHOD
Muddle kiwi fruit, and shake with other
ingredients. Strain into a martini glass
and garnish with a strawberry.

SDP
Martini glass

INGREDIENTS
30 ml Jaggard original
15 ml Licor 43
15 ml butterscotch schnapps
1 tsp thickened cream
strawberry to garnish

METHOD
Shake all ingredients and
double-strain into a martini
glass. Garnish with a strawberry.

GOLDEN CADILLAC
Champagne flute

INGREDIENTS
30 ml Galliano
60 ml white crème de cacao
30 ml light cream

METHOD
Combine all ingredients with ½ cup
crushed ice in an electric blender.
Blend at low speed for ten seconds.
Strain into a Champagne flute and serve.

BRANDY ALEXANDER

Champagne flute

INGREDIENTS
30 ml dark crème de cacao
30 ml brandy
splash of cream
ground nutmeg to garnish

METHOD
Combine ingredients with ice and
blend. Strain into a Champagne flute
and garnish with a sprinkle of nutmeg.

GIUSEPPE HABIT

Martini glass

INGREDIENTS
twist of lemon
45 ml Galliano
20 ml Frangelico
30 ml Cointreau
60 ml apple juice
2 twists of lemon to garnish

METHOD
Twist lemon into shaker, combine with
other ingredients and shake. Strain into
a martini glass and garnish with twists
of lemon.

LOUISIANA SLING
Highball glass

INGREDIENTS

45 ml absinth
30 ml lemon juice
15 ml sugar syrup
15 ml Cointreau
60 ml pineapple juice
wedge of lemon to garnish

METHOD
Shake and strain all ingredients
into a highball glass with crushed ice.
Garnish with a wedge of lemon.

BELLINI COCKTAIL
Champagne flute

INGREDIENTS

30 ml peach nectar
½ tsp lemon juice
30 ml peach schnapps
45 ml Champagne

METHOD
Mix the peach nectar, lemon juice and
schnapps in a chilled flute. Add crushed
ice, stir, and add Champagne.

COUTURE FIZZ
Champagne flute

INGREDIENTS
5 ml Campari
10 ml black raspberry liqueur
2 strawberries or raspberries
dash of lemon juice
dash of sugar syrup
130 ml Champagne
slice of strawberry to garnish

METHOD
Combine all ingredients (except
Champagne) in a mixing glass.
Chill, shake and double-strain into
a flute. Layer with Champagne and
float a strawberry slice.

PEAR & CARDAMON SIDECAR
Martini glass

INGREDIENTS
7 pods of green cardamon
30 ml Cointreau
20 ml pear liqueur
30 ml lemon juice
30 ml cognac
slice of pear to garnish

METHOD
Break away shells of cardamon pods
and muddle seeds in base of shaker.
Add all ingredients, shake and
double-strain into a martini glass.
Garnish with a fanned pear slice.

NAPOLI ICED TEA
Pilsner glass

INGREDIENTS

2 chunks of lemon
5 chunks of orange
30 ml Vanilla-Infused Rosso
20 ml Cointreau
10 ml vanilla liqueur
30 ml orange juice
30 ml red fruits tea
10 ml sugar syrup
slices of orange and lemon to garnish

METHOD

Muddle fruit and combine with other
ingredients. Shake and strain into
a pilsner glass. Garnish with orange
and lemon slices.

BANGKOK ICED TEA
Highball glass

INGREDIENTS

3 leaves of Italian basil
3 wedges of lime
6 mint leaves
10 ml dry vermouth
50 ml basil-infused Cinzano Bianco
splash of lemon and ginger tea
splash of ginger beer

METHOD

Muddle basil and lime. Add mint, alcohol
and ice, then shake. Pour into a highball
glass. Top with lemon and ginger tea
(cold) and ginger beer.

FRENCH PASSION
Old-fashioned glass

INGREDIENTS
50 ml cognac
30 ml vanilla liqueur
15 ml passionfruit liqueur
30 ml lemon juice
dash of vanilla essence
1 passionfruit to garnish
wheel of lemon to garnish

METHOD
Shake and strain all ingredients into
an old-fashioned glass. Garnish with
passionfruit pulp and a lemon wheel.

AFFOGATO – FRENCH STYLE
Old-fashioned glass

INGREDIENTS
2 scoops of vanilla ice cream
30 ml Cointreau
30 ml cognac
1 espresso shot

METHOD
Spoon the ice cream into a large
old-fashioned glass. Top with alcohol
and finish with a shot of espresso.
Serve with a teaspoon.

RINKY DINK SPECIAL
Martini glass

INGREDIENTS
30 ml apricot brandy
30 ml fresh lemon juice
10 ml Cointreau
10 ml Galliano
dash of sugar syrup
twist of orange to garnish

METHOD
Shake all ingredients and pour
into a martini glass. Garnish with
an orange twist.

FREUDIAN SLIP
Absinth glass

INGREDIENTS
15 ml absinth
15 ml Benedictine
15 ml green apple liqueur
15 ml lemon juice
15 ml cloudy apple juice
apple sherbet to garnish

METHOD
Shake all ingredients with ice and pour
into apple-sherbet-crusted absinth glass.

HEAVENLY HIBISCUS
Highball glass

INGREDIENTS
45 ml cognac
20 ml vanilla liqueur
15 ml hibiscus cordial
15 ml lemon juice
60 ml apple juice
dash of sugar syrup
wedge of green apple to garnish

METHOD
Shake all ingredients and serve
long into a chilled highball glass.
Garnish with a speared apple wedge.

BETWEEN THE SHEETS
Tumbler

INGREDIENTS
30 ml brandy
15 ml light rum
15 ml triple sec
splash of sweet and sour mix

METHOD
Pour brandy, rum and triple sec into
an ice-filled tumbler. Fill with sweet
and sour mix and serve.

rock around the clock

♥

Rock 'n' roll and fashion have always shaken hands, done deals and helped each other along the way. That's why I've dedicated a chapter to them – my strongest loves of all. This cavalcade of drinks has been especially created for this book to suit your drinking and listening moods.

Where rock'n'roll brings out the inner wild child in us all, fashion helps us keep it neatly stitched together. After all, what does it matter if you're dancing wildly to a Motörhead song in a gorgeous Prada knit, killer heels and a $400 skirt with vintage clutch bag?

Bad boys like Bon Scott, Mick Jagger and Jimi Hendrix showed us their outlaw ways as rock icons, and they also showed us that there are two kinds of men in the world – those who stick around and those who don't. Unfortunately, they belonged to the latter. If you find yourself hanging on to these blokes, then at the very least, drink to their honour but don't succumb to their spell.

While you're toasting, raise a glass to couture and Hollywood glamour. For that starlet fever, look no further than the va-va-voom of Marilyn Monroe and Coco Chanel. Choose an icon, down a cocktail and be transformed for a night!

COCO CHANEL
Martini glass

INGREDIENTS

15 ml white chocolate sauce
15 ml crème de cacao
15 ml crème de gingembre
20 ml cognac
20 ml cream
20 ml milk
white chocolate powder to garnish

METHOD

Shake all ingredients and pour into
a martini glass dusted with white
chocolate powder.

Coco Chanel embodied style; she showed us the
purpose of that little black dress in the back of our
wardrobes. So pull out your best black number and
drink to the French queen of style and sophistication.

NICO

Martini glass

INGREDIENTS

30 ml peach schnapps
30 ml Tuaca
30 ml pineapple juice
15 ml guava juice
**dash of grenadine and fruit-tea flakes
    to garnish**

METHOD

Shake all ingredients vigorously.
Strain into a chilled martini glass.
(It should have a thick foamy surface.)
To garnish, sprinkle a tiny amount of
grenadine to form an abstract pattern
on top and spoon a few fruit-tea flakes
in the centre. (The garnish is only
effective if the tea and grenadine sit
firmly on the surface.)

*Nico became one of the most intriguing fringe
figures of the rock scene in the late 60s.
She was a diva who rose to fame as a European
supermodel and also performed in Fellini's*
La Dolce Vita *and started to hang out with
the Velvet Underground. This collaboration
came about thanks to pop artist Andy Warhol,
who encouraged her to be an occasional singer
with the band.*

MARILYN MONROE
Martini glass

INGREDIENTS

20 ml honey dew liqueur
20 ml Malibu
15 ml cognac
30 ml lemon juice
10 ml sugar syrup
10 ml black raspberry liqueur
apple to garnish

METHOD

Pour all ingredients into a martini glass, stir, and garnish with skewered apple.

She once said, 'Sex is part of nature. I go along with nature.' Marilyn Monroe personified Hollywood glamour; she was a 50s sex goddess, a movie star who was much adored. She was synonymous with beauty, style and grace, and died at the age of 36. Her grandiosity lives on; drink this in honour of her.

MAE WEST
Highball glass

INGREDIENTS

30 ml rum
15 ml amaretto
15 ml blackberry liqueur
50 ml pineapple juice
2 cherries to garnish

METHOD

Shake and strain all ingredients into a highball glass. Garnish with 2 cherries on a toothpick.

Mae West was a Hollywood sex symbol for 50 years and earned her stripes working as an actor on Broadway. She was born in Brooklyn in 1893 and became known for that sultry voice, perfect hourglass figure and irreverent style. She died in LA in 1980.

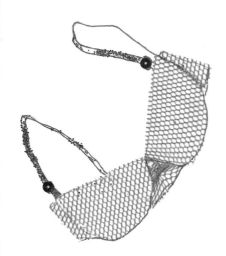

DOLLY PARTON
Tumbler

INGREDIENTS
30 ml Absolut Mandarin
15 ml Southern Comfort
15 ml butterscotch schnapps
20 ml lemon juice
60 ml white cranberry juice

METHOD
Shake and strain all ingredients
into a tumbler.

*For a bosom full of love, look no further than
the peroxide-blonde goddess of country music
— Dolly Parton. She's one part Barbie, two parts
woman. So when you've stopped working nine
to five, down this for refreshment.*

JOAN JETT
Highball glass

INGREDIENTS
3 wedges of lime
60 ml rum
splash of cola

METHOD
Squeeze lime wedges into a highball
glass, discarding the pieces. Build rum
and cola over ice.

*Joan Jett's signature anthem, 'I Love Rock 'n' Roll',
was belted out wearing a fitted black leather waist
jacket. She was an outlaw; she was sexy and she
rocked — first with her band The Runaways in the
70s and then with the Blackhearts in the 80s. This
drink is for rockers and rollers, pure and simple.*

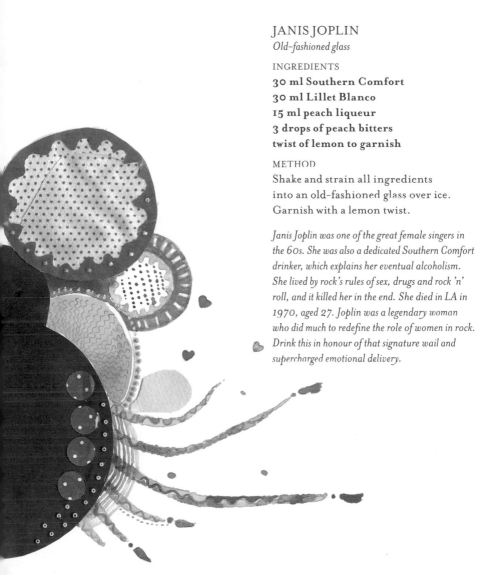

JANIS JOPLIN
Old-fashioned glass

INGREDIENTS
30 ml Southern Comfort
30 ml Lillet Blanco
15 ml peach liqueur
3 drops of peach bitters
twist of lemon to garnish

METHOD
Shake and strain all ingredients
into an old-fashioned glass over ice.
Garnish with a lemon twist.

*Janis Joplin was one of the great female singers in
the 60s. She was also a dedicated Southern Comfort
drinker, which explains her eventual alcoholism.
She lived by rock's rules of sex, drugs and rock 'n'
roll, and it killed her in the end. She died in LA in
1970, aged 27. Joplin was a legendary woman
who did much to redefine the role of women in rock.
Drink this in honour of that signature wail and
supercharged emotional delivery.*

BON SCOTT
Highball glass

INGREDIENTS
1 fig
½ lime
1 tsp brown sugar
60 ml rum
splash of ginger beer
slice of fig to garnish

METHOD
Muddle fig, lime and sugar, then churn
with crushed ice and rum. Pour into
a highball glass. Top with ginger beer.
Garnish with a slice of fig.

*Bon Scott personified everything that was sexily
rebellious. It didn't get more primal or sexually
motivated than Scott, who joined AC/DC as a
front man for five years. He was a legend, breaking
many hearts as he shagged his way around town.
His most famous quote: 'It keeps you fit — the alcohol,
nasty women, sweat on stage, bad food — it's all
very good for you.' He died in 1980, aged 33.*

GINNY HENDRIX
Martini glass

INGREDIENTS
4 wedges of lime
1 tsp sugar
60 ml gin
15 ml white crème de cacao
chocolate powder to garnish

METHOD
Muddle lime and sugar. Add gin,
crème de cacao and crushed ice to fill.
Serve in a martini glass dusted with
chocolate powder.

*Jimi Hendrix redefined cool in the late 60s with his
unique self-taught guitar-playing ways. He was
a shy fellow but a sexy one. He oozed charm and
charisma and put a new spin on rock fashion. His
appeal was embodied in the sexy sounds he created
through sweaty rock, funk and soul. Long live the
master who told us, 'The story of life is quicker than
the blink of an eye, the story of love is hello, goodbye.'*

SID VICIOUS
Martini glass

INGREDIENTS
75 ml vodka
5 ml sauvignon blanc
1 passionfruit
maraschino cherry to garnish

METHOD
Fill glass with ice. In a shaker, combine ice, vodka and wine, and double-strain into a martini glass. Drizzle passionfruit pulp into glass and garnish with a safety-pin skewered cherry.

Oh, what a figure of British punk rock we have here. It was all about anarchy and nihilism for this little punk rock boy who believed in taking everything to extremes. He was a rebel with a cause, but his junkie lifestyle couldn't hold him together for very long. Sid Vicious embodied everything that was disaffected and angst-driven in London in the 70s. We've all dated a guy like this — the one who isn't worth chasing any longer, but was definitely fun to chase in the beginning.

MICK JAGGARD
Martini glass

INGREDIENTS
2 squeezes of lime
45 ml Jaggard original
15 ml Cointreau
45 ml cranberry juice
twist of lime to garnish

METHOD
Shake and strain all ingredients into a martini glass. Garnish with a lime twist.

Mick Jagger once said, 'It's all right letting yourself go, as long as you can get yourself back.' That he has well and truly done, from mad drug days in the late 60s to rocking the panties off many a woman, even at age 60. He's dated the finest, from Marianne Faithfull to Jerry Hall. Drink this in celebration of the man who gave this quote: 'Anything worth doing is worth overdoing.'

ACKNOWLEDGEMENTS

I want to thank Kirsten Abbott for approaching me with the idea for this book and for making it happen. Thanks to Emma Schwarcz at Hardie Grant who took on the project midway and encouraged me wholeheartedly, and especially for being so damn fussy to make sure all measurements were completely accurate!

Thanks to my partner Billy Walsh and the Cherry Bar entourage (you know who you are, you maniacs who don't believe in measuring ingredients! Osker and Nat especially, you crazy cats).

To my friends Helen Razer and Susan King and to my dear friend Monica Levy, who helped me with all those gorgeous Sydney bars and hunted down the best bartenders for unique recipes — the tequila chapter is dedicated to you, babe!

To my mum and dad, need I say more, your support is endless.

To my editors at *The Age*, *Sydney Sun Herald*, *West Australian* and *NW* (Tiffany Dunk), who have supported me throughout my writing career.

Other very special thanks go to the legendary talents of bartenders who supplied such gorgeous recipes for this book: Grant Collins from the Water Bar, W Hotel; Mark Ward from Hugo's Group, founder of Yakusan; Mike Enright from The Loft Sydney; Matthew Bax from Der Raum Melbourne; Simon Page from Transport Public Bar; Cleo Seaman from The Como Hotel; Daniel Rosette from Terra Firma Northcote; Marcus Motteram from ffour; Murray Pitman from The Gin Palace; Tony Starr's Kitten Club; Phoenix; Misty Bar; Hairy Canary; and Café Pacifico Sydney.

Other inspiration comes from music, from the Supersuckers to Motörhead — do yourself a favour and find yourself some decent music to get wasted to!

INDEX

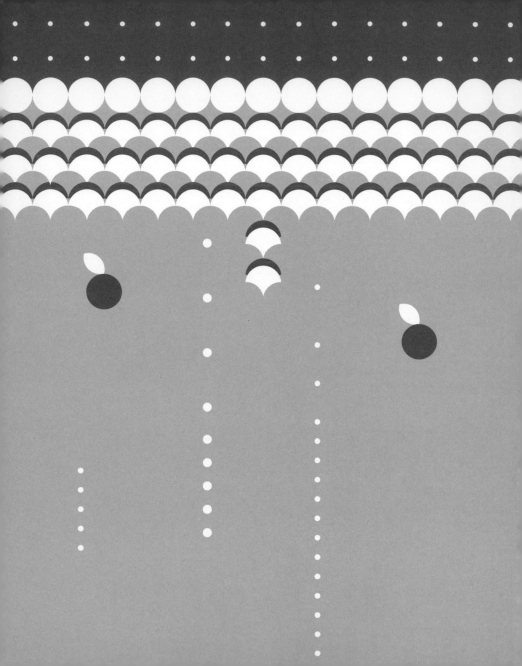